LIFEWAYS

The Comanche

RAYMOND BIAL

BENCHMARK BOOKS

MARSHALL CAVENDISH
NEW YORK

SERIES CONSULTANT: JOHN BIERHORST

ACKNOWLEDGMENTS

This book would not have been possible without the generous help of many individuals and organizations that have dedicated themselves to honoring the traditions of the Comanche. I am grateful to the friendly people of Oklahoma who helped me in making photographs, including Morina Scarborough, Ray Alabama, George F. Moran, Charles Chibitty, and Carolyn McBride. I am especially indebted to Marie Chebahtah who welcomed me to the Comanche Reservation and invited me to the Comanche Nation Fair in nearby Cache. I would like to thank everyone at Indian City U.S.A., the Southern Plains Indian Museum, and the Museum of the Great Plains for permission to photograph at their sites. I would also like to acknowledge the assistance of the National Archives, the Library of Congress, and the Philbrook Museum for a number of illustrations for *The Comanche*.

I would like to thank my editor, Kate Nunn, and Doug Sanders for their good humor and hard work in guiding this book and others in the *Lifeways* series from concept to finished manuscript. I am indebted as well to John Bierhorst for his many insights and helpful suggestions in reviewing the work-in-progress. As always, I thank my wife, Linda, and my children, Anna, Sarah, and Luke, for their faithful support of my work—including our week-long photo shoot in Oklahoma during which temperatures soared to 112 degrees every day.

Benchmark Books
Marshall Cavendish Corporation
99 White Plains Road, Tarrytown, New York 10591-9001
Text copyright © 2000 by Raymond Bial
Map copyright © 2000 by the Marshall Cavendish Corporation
Map by Rodica Prato

Library of Congress Cataloging-in-Publication Data
Bial, Raymond.
The Comanche / Raymond Bial.
p. cm. – (Lifeways)
Includes bibliographical references.
Summary: Discusses the history, culture, social structure, beliefs, and notable people of the Comanche Indians.
ISBN 0-7614-0864-9 (lib. bdg.)
1. Comanche Indians—History—Juvenile literature. 2. Comanche Indians—Social life and customs—Juvenile literature. [1. Comanche Indians. 2. Indians of North America.] I. Title. II. Series: Bial, Raymond. Lifeways.
E99.C85B53 2000 978.0049745—dc21 99-24133 CIP
Printed in Italy
6 5 4 3 2

Cover photos: Raymond Bial

The photographs in this book are used by permission and through the courtesy of: The Philbrook Museum of Art, Tulsa, Oklahoma: 1, 16, 33, 36, 53, 55, 90. Raymond Bial: 6, 8-9, 15, 19, 20-21, 24-25, 39, 40 (top), 42-43, 52, 56, 57, 63, 64, 73, 74 (top & bottom), 76-77, 79, 80, 86-87, 89, 100-101, 102-103, 105, 107, 108-109. National Museum of American Art, Washington, D.C./Art Resource, NY: 29, 30-31, 40 (bottom), 48, 69. The Pierpont Morgan Library/Art Resource, NY: 45. Art Resource, NY: 70-71. Library of Congress: 94-95, 97, 98. Amon Carter Museum, Fort Worth, Texas: 113. Americans for Indian Opportunity: 114.

This book is respectfully dedicated
to all the people who have devoted
themselves to keeping alive the
spirit of the Comanche.

Contents

Author's Note

AT THE DAWN OF THE TWENTIETH CENTURY, NATIVE Americans were thought to be a vanishing race. However, despite four hundred years of warfare, deprivation, and disease, American Indians have not gone away. Countless thousands have lost their lives, but over the course of this century the populations of native tribes have grown tremendously. Even as American Indians struggle to adapt to modern Western life, they have also kept the flame of their traditions alive—the language, religion, stories, and the everyday ways of life. An exhilarating renaissance in Native American culture is now sweeping the nation from coast to coast.

The *Lifeways* books depict the social and cultural life of the major nations, from the early history of native peoples in North America to their present-day struggles for survival and dignity. Historical and contemporary photographs of traditional subjects, as well as period illustrations, are blended throughout each book so that readers may gain a sense of family life in a tipi, a hogan, or a longhouse.

No single book can comprehensively portray the intricate and varied lifeways of an entire tribe, or nation. I only hope that young people will come away with a deeper appreciation for the rich tapestry of Indian culture—both then and now—and a keen desire to learn more about these first Americans.

1. Origins

When the Comanche acquired horses, their way of life changed dramatically. They soon became expert riders and counted the horse among their prized possessions.

SUPERB HORSEMEN, GREAT WARRIORS, AND SKILLED BUFFALO HUNTERS, to many the Comanche (cuh MAN chee) have come to represent strength, courage, and endurance. Along with their prowess on horseback and their bravery in battle, they have long endured the hardships of extreme weather—the deep snows of bitter winters, the blinding sleet of spring and fall, and the baking heat of summer, along with occasional flash floods, droughts, and deadly tornadoes. At times they have also suffered terrible hunger and thirst while wandering the southern plains in what are now the states of Texas and Oklahoma.

Yet the Comanche are a deeply spiritual people as well, with a firm faith in the Great Spirit and a belief in an afterlife. They consider themselves to be a very small part of a large universe, and they draw their own strong medicine, or personal power, from the spirits around them. Young men "make medicine," or seek their personal power, when they go on their first vision quest. Throughout their lives, they measure spiritual power in terms of good or strong medicine and weak, bad, or unlucky medicine.

Comanche beliefs are vividly reflected in stories of their origin. Other stories recount the mischief of Coyote, the wisdom and generosity of the people, and the constant struggle of the Comanche to survive. The following story is about a little girl and a lovely flower. Because the buffalo were so fond of the tender green leaves of this flower, some people called it buffalo clover. To others, it was wolf flower or *el conejo*, "the rabbit." To the settlers, the flowers resembled the bonnets worn by women to shade their faces from the blazing Texas sun. And the flower—now the state flower of Texas—came to be known as the bluebonnet. Here's how it came to be.

"The Legend of the Bluebonnet"

Long ago, the Comanche people were as numerous as the grass on the southern prairies. Every spring they danced, sang, and prayed to the Great Spirit for the rains to fall and the great herds of buffalo to graze nearby. However, one spring there came a drought, which lasted through the summer, and the land turned to dust. That winter ice and snow swept over the land. Even far to the south, the woods and grasses of the coastal plains were glazed with silvery ice.

All the game, including the buffalo, died or fled. The people became thin and weak, and many starved to death. Then a dreadful disease—smallpox—broke out and many parents, grandparents, and children died. People were now certain that the Great Spirit was displeased and had turned away from them. Day and night, the medicine men chanted, danced to the music of the sacred drums, slashed their bodies, and prayed to the Great Spirit, asking why he had brought such suffering to the people.

At last the Great Spirit answered the prayers of the medicine men. He explained that the people had become selfish. They had taken much from Mother Earth and given little in return. As atonement they must burn the one possession that was most precious to them. The ashes from this sacrifice must then be offered to the four winds—east and west, north and south.

Anxiously, the warriors gathered about the fire. "Certainly the Great Spirit couldn't mean my horse," one of the men pronounced.

"He could not want my prize bow," another stated.

"Surely, the Great Spirit does not expect me to give up my lovely buffalo robe," cried a young woman.

The people had so little and no one wished to give up anything, especially their most cherished blanket or weapon.

Kneeling in the shadows among the warriors and women was a little girl, known as She-Who-Is-Alone, who had lost her family to hunger and disease. Hidden in the folds of her tattered dress was her only possession—a cornhusk doll made by her mother and decorated by her father. She lovingly clutched the doll, with its sweet eyes, mouth, and nose painted on with the juice of wild berries. Dressed in a buckskin skirt, mantle, headband, and moccasins, the doll had long black braids made from gleaming strands of horsehair. Tied in the doll's hair was the vivid blue feather of the tattletale bird that sings "Jay! Jay!" from the highest branches of the tallest tress.

She-Who-Is-Alone adored her cornhusk doll as a mother loves her baby. For the rest of the day and long into the night, she held her doll close to her heart and listened to the people squabbling among themselves, making excuses for not sacrificing their property. When everyone had finally returned to the warmth of their lodges and drifted into sleep, She-Who-Is-Alone rose from her bed, lit a torch at the fire, and slipped into the night.

Wiping the tears from her eyes, she walked to a high hill not far from the camp. Climbing to the highest point, she made a fire of twigs and grass. Then, as the fire flickered orange and yellow in the night, she closed her eyes and cast her beloved doll into the flames. Opening her eyes, she watched it burn until it was gray ashes. Carefully scooping the ashes in the hollow of her hand, with great dignity, She-Who-Is-Alone scattered them to the east and to the west, then to the north and to the south. As soon as she had made her offering, she noticed that a lovely blue flower was blooming where the fire had once burned.

So deep was her grief over the loss of her doll that She-Who-Is-Alone could not walk back to the camp. She lay down on the hill, curling up in the grass, and slept there for the rest of the night. When she awoke at first light, she saw the rolling hills were blanketed with blue flowers. Each had tender green leaves and a flower as deeply blue as the feathers of the tattletale bird that cries "Jay! Jay!" at the top of the trees.

Rising with the morning sun, all the people of the camp walked to the top of the hill and gathered in awe around She-Who-Is-Alone. They were amazed at the sprawling fields of blue flowers. They had never seen such lovely blossoms flowing end-lessly in the four directions of the winds. At the sight of the blue flowers the medicine men declared that the wish of the Great Spirit had been nobly honored.

A veil of rain soon descended over the plains, the rolling waves of grass were renewed, and the trees burst forth with green leaves. The buffalo and the other four-leggeds returned to the land of the Comanche, as did the birds of the air. The people rejoiced and held a great feast in honor of the girl. Every spring since that day, the Great Spirit remembers the sacrifice of the little girl by blanketing the hills and valleys of Texas with blue flowers. This is the sign that the rains will be coming once again. And the little girl was given a new name: She-Who-Dearly-Loves-Her-People.

LIKE ALL THE NATIVE PEOPLES OF NORTH AMERICA, THE ANCESTORS OF the Comanches came from Siberia thousands of years ago, most likely following herds of wild animals across the narrow land bridge that then connected Asia and Alaska. Eventually settling in the central Northwest near the upper reaches of the Platte River in present-day Wyoming, the Comanches were originally part of the Shoshone, or Snake people. Hunters and gatherers, for hundreds of years they made their homes in bark lodges deep in the forests among the mountain slopes and valleys.

They lived on game and wild plants. In the forest, the men stalked deer, rabbits, and other small animals while women gathered roots, berries, and seeds. Occasionally, the men killed a buffalo—at that time the large, shaggy beasts roamed freely as far west as the Rocky Mountains. When game became scarce, the band moved to another part of the forest.

After they migrated south, the Comanche became buffalo hunters. Racing along on horseback, they drove spears or shot arrows into the powerful animals.

The Comanche came to rely on the buffalo for nearly all their basic needs—food, clothing, and shelter—especially after they had acquired horses in the 1600s and were better able to pursue the massive herds. Horses were first brought to North America by the Spanish in 1519. The Spanish tried to keep the Indians from acquiring the graceful, powerful animals, but eventually a few horses were stolen. Over time, Native Americans also traded for

This 1970 painting by Rance Hood entitled Untamed Hearts *captures the pride and independence of the Comanche. Riding their spirited horses, they dominated the southern plains for generations.*

horses or captured animals that had gotten loose. Eventually all the Plains Indians had mounts. Around A.D. 1680, after they too had acquired horses, the Comanches split from the Shoshone and drifted southward out of the forests, settling in an area between the Platte and Arkansas Rivers in what is now eastern Colorado and western Kansas. Here, they made their home for about fifty years. Then one of the bands began moving south again, and by 1830 the other bands had followed.

Speaking a language in the Shoshonean linguistic family, which includes the Shoshone, Bannock, Paiute, and Ute, the Comanche called themselves *Nermernuh*, or *Nerm*, meaning "people of the people." The word *Comanche* most likely comes from the Ute term for the tribe, *Kwuma-ci* or *Koh-Mahts*, meaning "enemy," which the Spanish spelled as *Komántcia*.

While the Shoshone continued to live as hunters and gatherers in the evergreen forests, the Comanche transformed themselves into Plains Indians—skilled horsemen, buffalo hunters, and warriors. The only Shoshonean-speaking people to leave the Rocky Mountains, the Comanches fiercely battled the Apache, Kiowa, and other Indian tribes of the southern plains.

By 1750, with a nation twenty to thirty thousand strong, the Comanche had firmly established themselves in the heart of the southern plains, a region they would dominate for well over a century. The finest horsemen on the continent, they defended their vast lands against native peoples and invading Spaniards and Americans. With their fast, sturdy horses, they could hunt down enough buffalo in a single day to feed their families for months. War parties of young warriors had the freedom to raid homesteads all across the Texas frontier. Tearing across the prairie, swift as the wind on their fine horses, their faces streaked with black warpaint, they struck terror into the hearts of native enemies, settlers, and the blue-coated cavalrymen sent to stop them.

The People and the Land

A nomadic people, the Comanche have lived in many places. During the 1740s they moved south across the Arkansas River to the edge of what came to be known as the Llano Estacado, or Staked Plains. For generations, the Comanche have lived on these stretches of prairie—shimmering grasslands that flow like waves upon the open sea, interrupted only by an occasional cluster of ragged mountains or a jagged streambed with a silver vein of water trickling through it. Otherwise, the country was marked in each direction only by the four winds, an overwhelming sky, and hardly a single obstruction in sight. One could easily get lost here, the land so flat and barren that stakes had to be driven into the ground to mark the trails.

The Comanche so thoroughly dominated the territory of western Oklahoma and Texas that the region became known as the Comanchería. Extending south from the foothills of the Rocky Mountains and the Arkansas River through central Texas to the present-day city of San Antonio, the Comanchería also spread

Much of Comanche territory was a vast, treeless plain. Despite long, dry summers and bitterly cold winters, the wandering people thrived in this land.

The Comanche depended on the buffalo for food, clothing, and shelter. They made use of virtually every part of the burly animals, not only their flesh and organs, but their hide, hooves, and bones.

west to the Edwards Plateau and the Pecos River in New Mexico. It was a country made for great horsemen. Here, a warrior could ride for hundreds of miles, all the way to the Gulf of Mexico, with nothing to hinder him.

The land was also noted for its extreme weather. Cold winds swept over the bare plains, along with driving snow and sleet that chilled people to the bone. Here, one could get lost in the swirling white wall of a blizzard, and freeze to death in no time. The other half of the year was marked by a breathlessly hot summer. There were long months of drought, the grass brittle and brown when the buffalo headed north in search of greener prairies. Yet the plains also had their softer moods; they were home to the tender green of spring, the occasional radiance of summer, and the golden light of autumn.

Millions of the snorting buffalo once darkened these plains for as far as the eye could see. In the vast, open country, often with not a tree in sight, the Comanche felt an exhilarating sense of space and freedom as they galloped after the huge herds. But antelope, deer, elk, and other wild creatures also made their home in this rugged country. Out on the plains, birds tended nests carefully hidden in the sparse vegetation. Overhead vultures, hawks, and eagles circled, scanning the harsh, dry landscape for their next meal. There were whole towns of prairie dogs, the rodents popping out of their holes, then diving back down into their burrows with a flicker of their tails. Waddling along the dry ground, armadillos roved the mesquite, while the resourceful coyote, always keeping his distance, sniffed out rodents and ran down jackrabbits.

Until the first settlers arrived, the Comanches wandered here in scattered bands, battling the Apaches and allying with the Kiowas. When the trickle of land-hungry pioneers turned into a full-scale invasion, the Comanche went to war again defending not only their honor, but fighting for their land and their lives.

2. A Wandering People

The lives of the nomadic Comanche revolved around the tipi. Here, people gathered to eat meals, visit with each other, and tell stories by the fire.

THE COMANCHE SHARED A COMMON LANGUAGE, AND THEY VIEWED themselves as a single people. However, unlike the Sioux, Cheyenne, and other tribes that lived on the prairies from Texas to the Dakotas, they did not organize themselves into warrior societies and did not emphasize rituals such as the Sun Dance. As a nomadic people, they came to be loosely organized into several divisions, or bands—groups of family members that traveled and hunted together. Among the major divisions were the *Penateka*, or Honey Eaters, who first moved southward and later lived nearest the Texan and Mexican settlements. The *Noyeka* (Those Who Move Often), also known as the *Nokoni* (Those Who Turn Back), traveled more than any over group, primarily in the eastern portion of the Comanchería. "They always turned back before they got where they were going," said one Comanche man. Most likely, they weren't going anywhere in particular, but were instead drifting continually over the plains. The *Kotsoteka*, or Buffalo Eaters, lived to the north of the *Nokoni*, and the *Yamparika*, or Yap Eaters, the last group to break with the Shoshone, lived nearby. These people were so named because they ate the potato-like root of the yap, a wild plant of the plains. The last group, the *Quahadi*, or Antelope, lived in the west, near the present-day border of Texas and New Mexico. Other major divisions were the *Parkeenaum* (Water People), *Tenawa* (Those Who Stay Downstream), and *Tanima* (Liver Eaters).

Each division had its own government and leaders; they united only to fight a common enemy or to embark on a major raid.

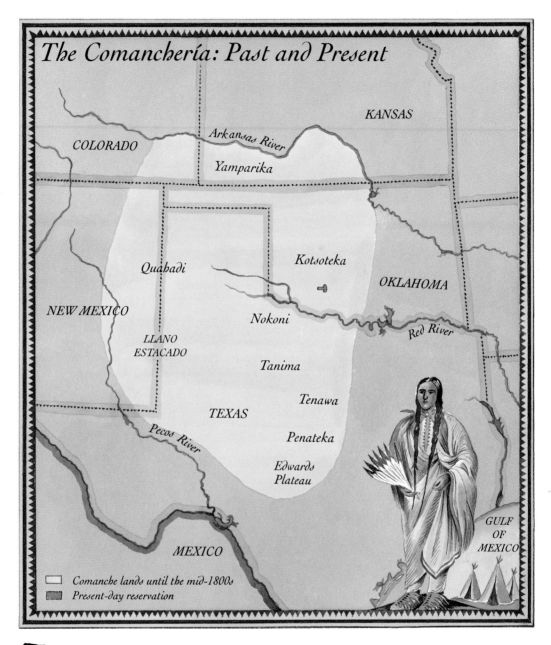

The Comancheria: Past and Present

KANSAS

COLORADO

Arkansas River

Yamparika

Quahadi

Kotsoteka

OKLAHOMA

NEW MEXICO

Nokoni

LLANO
ESTACADO

Red River

Tanima

Tenawa

TEXAS

Penateka

Pecos River

Edwards
Plateau

MEXICO

GULF
OF
MEXICO

Comanche lands until the mid-1800s
Present-day reservation

The Comanche once ranged over a vast area known as the Comanchería. Their territory stretched over grasslands and deserts from Western Oklahoma through the Texas Panhandle into New Mexico.

Each band was organized around its own council, which included all the men in the band. Since all decisions had to be unanimous, the council often met for long sessions until it reached a consensus, or general agreement. If a warrior could not agree with a decision, he left the band. People did not have to remain in their own band and often moved from one group to another. Each band had a principal chief, along with a war chief and a peace chief. Leaders were selected, not by heredity, but for their wisdom, generosity, and bravery in battle. During raids, the war chief took charge of the band. Because the bands were so loosely organized, warriors could also form their own war parties for raids. The peace chief was usually a wise elder consulted by the members of the band but whose advice was often ignored.

Horsemen

Although the exact date is not known, by the late 1600s, the Comanche had certainly obtained horses, and by the early 1700s they had become remarkable horsemen. Thereafter, they stole the best horses from Spanish and Pueblo settlements or captured mustangs that had escaped and returned to the wilds. As traders, they brought the horse to the Cheyenne, Sioux, and other Plains Indians.

Like other Plains tribes, the Comanches originally relied heavily on dogs as beasts of burden. The dogs carried bundles on their backs and dragged a kind of sled called a travois (trav WAH).

As shown in this George Catlin painting entitled Comanche Feats of Horsemanship, *men were trained to ride their mounts at breakneck speeds into battle.*

Women strapped poles to a harness on either side of the dog's shoulders and tied folded tipi coverings and other belongings between the poles. The travois was far superior to wheels on the uneven ground of the mountains and prairie. When they obtained horses, the Comanches simply enlarged the harness and lengthened the poles, which enabled them to carry more substantial loads. Naming the animal *puc*, which means "horse," the

As seen in this painting by George Catlin entitled Comanche Moving Camp, Dog Fight en Route, *bands often fought with other tribes of the southern plains over prime hunting grounds.*

Comanche honored their new beast of burden as a god. Unlike the dog, the horse could live on grass, and during times of scarcity provide food. (Because of the taboo regarding the coyote, which was considered a sacred creature, the dog was not eaten.) The horse also provided skins for saddles, robes, shelters, and rawhide thongs. The hair of the mane and tail was woven into ropes and bridles.

The Comanche greatly admired horses, which were able to carry and pull much heavier loads than dogs could. The Comanche also traveled faster and farther on their swift horses— until the arrival of the horse few Native Americans wandered great distances over the plains. Men captured and broke wild horses but preferred to trade or steal horses that had already been broken. Stealing horses from another tribe became a daring sport among the Plains Indians. A successful raid brought status and war honors, and the size of a man's herd became a symbol of his wealth.

The Comanches relied upon the horse as a powerful force in hunting and waging war. They could now gallop alongside stampeding buffalo or race over hundreds of miles when making raids. Their skill as riders enabled the Comanche to move southward and repeatedly defeat the Spanish and Mexicans for over a century. Riding their swift mounts, the Comanches also swept down upon Texas settlers, brutally massacring the men, kidnapping women and children, and then fleeing any pursuers. The horse allowed the Comanche to battle the U.S. Army in a war that raged for years from the Arkansas River to the Mexican border.

When it came to horses the Comanche were the richest of all the Plains Indians—in most bands horses outnumbered people. With fewer than two thousand people, the Antelope band had around 15,000 horses and three to four hundred mules. By comparison, the entire Pawnee tribe had only 1,400 horses. Horses were the most important property and measure of wealth among the Comanches. Although a man might own a herd of hundreds of animals—one prominent chief owned 1,500 animals—each Comanche had a favorite horse that he kept picketed near his tipi. Killing a man's beloved horse was considered murder and had to be avenged. When a man died, his horse was often killed over his grave or given to his best friend.

Even before they could walk the Comanche learned to ride horses. As captured in Wind Spirit, *a 1955 painting by Blackbear Bosin, women and children were excellent riders.*

By the 1800s, millions of wild horses ranged throughout the American West. The Comanche captured these animals by driving them into a corral built near a water hole or by creasing a mustang. Only an expert marksman could crease an animal by shooting precisely through the neck muscle just above the spine without causing a serious injury. The horse fell paralyzed for a few minutes—just long enough for the shooter to cinch a rope around its neck. Men also ran down and lassoed the best of the wild horses. Sometimes, they waited until late winter when the cold weather and lack of food left the horses thin and weak—or late summer when the horses became so fat they had lost some of their speed. One of the best ways to ambush them was at a water hole when they had drunk their fill and were further slowed down.

Horses also became a primary means of exchange—a man might trade one or more of his horses for a good rifle. The Comanches traded their horses to the Cheyenne and other tribes for guns, blankets, kettles, calico, and beads. However, the Comanche preferred to steal horses in raids—a man was highly honored for his ability to quietly crawl into a herd late at night and lead away the sleekest horses without being noticed by any of the armed guards. Even when the horses were hobbled, or had their legs tied together, and confined in a stable of heavy timbers, the Comanches could slip in unnoticed and artfully, as if by magic, take the best mounts. The owner of a large herd was highly respected for his skill and daring in capturing the animals. Generosity was among the highest virtues of the Comanche, and it was considered especially gracious to give a fine horse to a friend.

The Comanche language had many words for horses, depending mainly on their color, including *dupsikuma* (a brown horse), *duukuma* (a black horse), *ohaieka* (a light bay-colored horse), and many other variations. A *dunnia* was a yellow horse with a black mane and tail. War ponies, racehorses, and personal horses were named, while most of the herd was not. "Paints," or pintos, were especially prized among horse breeders, who kept only pinto stallions. The Comanche became expert breeders, producing the finest animals for war, hunting, and sport. Horse races were a favorite pastime, with men often betting on the outcome.

Everyone in the family rode horses. Young children were strapped to a gentle old mare—even before they could walk—and women had riding horses as well as pack animals. By age four or five, both girls and boys were expert riders, yet, as a warrior and buffalo hunter, a boy was also expected to become a trick rider. His highest obligation as a warrior was to rescue fallen warriors, never leaving a comrade to be stripped, scalped, or mutilated. Day after day, year after year, he learned to snatch objects from the ground while riding at full speed. He learned to dance upon his horse's back while the animal galloped under him. Riding bareback, holding only a loop of rope, he learned to cling to the side of his horse, which became his shield as he shot arrows with deadly accuracy under the neck and belly.

Buffalo Hunters

To find the sprawling herds of buffalo, people followed the horned toad, whose Comanche name means "asking about the buffalo," or they watched the ravens, who often followed the herds to eat the insects on their hides. If a raven circled the camp four times, the Comanche believed it was telling the people that buffalo were nearby. Using spears and arrows, the Comanche usu-

In this 1942 painting by L. Dick entitled Buffalo Chase, *two men ride, lances in hand, alongside a group of buffalo. To bring down the large beasts, they thrust spears into their hearts and lungs.*

ally swept down on the huge sea of fat buffalo in large group hunts that involved the entire band—a serious and dangerous, but also thrilling, undertaking. Riding their well-trained horses, men raced alongside a buffalo and either shot an arrow or thrust a spear into its body, aiming for the heart or lungs. Boys took part in the big hunts not long after they learned to ride horses. Serving as water boys and fire keepers, they learned by watching their fathers gallop after the stampeding buffalo. Killing his first buffalo was a defining event in the life of a teenage boy. Afterward, his father held a feast in his honor, and the boy received many gifts. He might also receive a new name to acknowledge his courageous deed.

The Comanche used nearly every part of the buffalo. Little was ever wasted because, like the eagle and the coyote, these animals were sacred. After the hunt, the women skinned and butchered the chunky bodies strewn over the plains. Everyone had plenty of fresh meat—the liver and other organs that spoiled quickly in the heat were eaten right away. As a delicacy, the liquid was poured from the gall bladder over the raw liver and devoured with relish. The Comanche especially favored the entrails and the marrow of the bones. Only the heart was not eaten, because the herds symbolically lived forever through the steady beat of this organ. If he was thirsty, a man might drink the warm blood of the buffalo.

Everyone shared the meat. Giving was very important to the Comanche, especially for those who were the most skillful hunters and warriors. The delicious tongue, hump meat, and ribs were cooked that day, but much of the fresh meat was packed on travois and toted back to camp. There, women cut the red meat into thin strips, which were hung on racks to dry in the sun. Most of the dried meat was then stored for the lean months of winter. Sometimes women pounded the dried meat, called jerky, and mixed it with berries and fat to make pemmican, a food men ate when they were off on raids and war parties. The hides and bones were set aside for making tipis, tools, and perhaps a few treasured toys.

Tipis

Like other Plains Indians, the Comanche lived in cone-shaped tipis. The basic structure consisted of poles, each about fourteen feet long, made from slender pine or cedar trees peeled, seasoned, and pared down to the appropriate width. To set up the frame, women tied four of the poles together, set the frame upright, and spread out the legs. They next placed from twelve to thirty smaller poles around the frame—but twenty-two was the average.

The Comanche sheathed their tipis with a covering made of buffalo hides sewn together. To prepare the fresh buffalo hides, women first spread them out on the ground and scraped away the fat and flesh with bone or antler blades. Then they left the hides out in the sun. After the hides had dried, they next scraped off the thick hair, and then soaked them in water. After several days, to soften the hides they vigorously rubbed in a mixture of animal fat, brains, and liver. The hides were made even more supple by fur-

Women scraped the flesh from buffalo hides then stretched them out to dry in the sun. The rawhide was used to make shields, moccasin soles, and other useful articles, or it was worked into supple buckskin.

The flaps at the top of the tipi could be opened to create a draft, which drew out the smoke from cook fires. During rain or heavy snow, the flap could be closed with a long pole.

Comanche Village, Women Dressing Robes and Drying Meat, *by George Catlin.*

ther rinsing and working them back and forth over a rawhide thong. Finally, they were smoked over a fire, which gave them a light tan color.

To finish the tipi covering, women laid out the tanned hides side by side and stitched them together. As many as twenty-two hides could be used, but fourteen was the average. When finished, the hide covering was tied to a pole and raised, wrapped around the cone-shaped frame, and pinned together with pencil-sized wooden skewers. Two wing-shaped flaps at the top of the tipi were turned back to make an opening, which could be adjusted to keep out the wind and create a draft of air to draw away smoke. Always facing east toward the rising sun, the tipi doorway was covered with a hide flap. Some people decorated their tipis with stripes and geometric designs.

Tipis also had a buffalo hide "dew cloth" hung on the inside wall from about shoulder-height down to the damp ground. Dew cloths kept out moisture and held pockets of insulating air. With a fire burning in the center of the earthen floor, the tipis stayed warm in the winter. During the summer, the bottom edges could be rolled up to allow the cool breezes to drift over the people inside. Cooking was also done outside during the hot weather.

The tipi made a very practical home for a wandering people. Working together, several women could quickly set it up or take it down. So portable were the tipis that an entire band could be packed up and off chasing a buffalo herd in about fifteen minutes.

3. Lifeways

Since they traveled often, the Comanche did not use clay pottery, which was too fragile and easily broken. Instead, they stored food and personal belongings in sturdy rawhide pouches called parfleches.

Cycle of Life

COMANCHE BANDS WERE COMPOSED OF FAMILIES THAT INCLUDED CHILDREN, parents, and grandparents, as well as aunts and uncles. Large families were essential to survival because many people, including fathers and mothers, died in raids, warfare, and during buffalo hunts. Sickness and the hardships of daily life, including the brutal weather, also snatched away lives of the young and old alike. If the Comanche were to remain strong, they needed many people in the band. Newborns were welcomed and cherished not only by the family, but the entire band. If the family was harmed, through death or divorce, the children were still assured a place within the group. As they grew up, children were taught the customs and beliefs that had sustained many previous generations of their people.

Birth. If a woman gave birth while the band was in camp, she moved into a tipi, or a brush lodge if it was summer, and one or more of the older women assisted as midwives. Men were not allowed in the tipi during or immediately after the delivery. First, the midwives softened the earthen floor of the tipi and dug two holes—one for heating water and the other for the afterbirth. One or two stakes were driven into the ground near the expectant mother's bedding for her to grip during labor pains. Sage was burned as an offering. If a woman went into labor while the band was on the move, she simply paused along the trail, gave birth to her child, and after a few hours caught up with the group again.

Cradleboards were a practical way for busy mothers to look after their babies. Newborns were safely tucked into the cradleboards, where they spent much of their first year.

Both girls and boys were welcomed into the band. However, though girls would grow up and bear more children, boys were favored. If the baby was a boy, one of the midwives informed the father or grandfather, "It's your close friend." Families might paint a black spot on the flap of the tipi doorway to let others know that the tribe was strengthened with another warrior. After the birth, the midwives hung the umbilical cord from a hackberry tree; if it was not disturbed before it rotted, it was believed the child would enjoy a long and prosperous life.

The newborn was swaddled and remained with its mother in the tipi for a few days. The baby was then placed in a cradleboard, and the mother went back to work. She could easily carry her baby on her back or prop the cradleboard against a tree where the baby could watch her while she gathered seeds or roots. Cradleboards consisted of a flat board. Attached to the board was a kind of basket made from rawhide straps or a leather sheath that laced up the front. With soft dry moss as a diaper, the young one was safely tucked into the leather pocket. During cold weather, the baby was wrapped in blankets, then placed in the cradleboard. The baby remained in the cradleboard for about ten months, then was allowed to crawl around.

Sometimes, the father named his child, but he usually asked a medicine man or other person of distinction to do so in the hope of insuring a long and productive life for the child. During the public naming ceremony, the medicine man lit his pipe and offered smoke to the heavens, earth, and each of the four directions. He prayed that the child would remain happy and healthy. Then he lifted the child to symbolize its growing up and announced the child's name four times, holding the young one a little higher each time. The child's name foretold its future; even a weak or sickly child could grow up to be a great warrior, hunter, and raider, if given a name suggesting courage and strength.

Boys were often named after a grandfather, uncle, or other relative. Girls were usually named after one of the father's relatives, but the name was selected by the mother. As children grew up, they also acquired nicknames.

Childhood. The Comanche looked upon their children as their most precious gift—children were never whipped and rarely punished. Sometimes, though, an older sister or another relative was called upon to discipline a child, or the parents arranged for a bogey man to scare the youngster. Occasionally, old people donned sheets and frightened disobedient boys and girls. Children were also told about Big Cannibal Owl who lived in a cave on the south side of the Wichita Mountains and ate bad children at night.

Children learned from example by observing and listening to their parents and others in the band. As soon as she was old enough to walk, a girl followed her mother about the camp, playing at the daily tasks of cooking and making clothing. She was also very close to her mother's sisters, who were not called aunt, but *pia*, meaning mother. She was given a little deerskin doll,

*T*wo Comanche girls stand by their tipi in this painting by George Catlin. From their mothers and other women in the band, they learned the many skills needed to provide for their families.

which she took with her everywhere—just as her mother had carried her on her back. She learned to make all the clothing for the doll and lovingly dressed and tended to its every need.

A boy identified not only with his father but with his father's family, as well as the bravest warriors in the band. He learned to ride a horse before he could walk. By the time he was four or five he was expected to be able to skillfully handle a horse. When he was five or six, he was given a small bow and arrows. He was often taught to ride and shoot by his grandfather since his father and the other men were away on raids and hunts. His grandfather also told him of his own boyhood and taught him the history and legends of the Comanche.

As he grew older, he joined the other boys and hunted birds. He eventually ranged farther from camp in search of larger game. Encouraged to be a skilled hunter, he learned the signs of the prairie as he patiently and quietly stalked game. He became more self-reliant yet also grew up with many companions. They played together as a group, forming strong bonds and a sense of cooperation that they would need when they later rode together on raids and hunts.

Coming-of-Age. Boys were highly respected in the band, because they would become warriors and might very well die young in battle. As he approached manhood, a boy went on his first buffalo hunt. If he made a kill, his father honored him with a feast. Only after he had proven himself on a buffalo hunt was a young man allowed to go on the warpath.

When he was ready to become a warrior, at about age fifteen or sixteen, a young man first "made his medicine" by going on a vision quest. Following this quest, his father gave the young man a good horse to ride into battle and another mount for the trail. If he proved himself as a warrior, a Give Away Dance might be held in his honor. As drummers faced east, he and the other young men danced. His parents, as well as his other relatives and the people in the band, threw presents at his feet, especially blankets and horses symbolized by sticks. Anyone might snatch one of the gifts for themselves, although those with many possessions refrained—they did not wish to appear greedy. People often gave away all their belongings during these dances, providing for others in the band but leaving themselves with nothing.

Like her mother before her, a girl learned to gather berries, nuts, and roots. She carried water and collected wood, and when she was about twelve, she learned to cook meals, make tipis, sew clothing, and perform all the other tasks essential to becoming a wife and mother. She was then considered ready to be married.

When she had her first period, she went into confinement—and did so every month, during each menstrual cycle, throughout her childbearing years. If her husband had strong medicine—and every Comanche man thought he did—it was believed that her menstrual blood would weaken, even destroy, his great personal power. So, she retired to her own tipi or moved in with her parents, where she would not harm the already weakened medicine of the old.

Marriage. Boys might boldly risk their lives as hunters and warriors, but when it came to girls, they tended to be very bashful. However, they did like to show off in front of the girls. A boy might also visit a person gifted in love medicine who could charm the young woman into accepting him. During courtship, the girl often approached the boy. "Boys seemed to stay pretty much in their tipis," one man said. "It was the girl's place to come to them."

A boy, however, might approach a girl as she went for wood or water. But since they were not supposed to be seen together, they often met in secret, slipping out together at night.

When he wished to marry, a boy offered a gift—usually one or more horses—to the girl's father or guardian. He might also agree to work as a hunter and raider for her family for two or three years. Usually, the young man asked an uncle or friend to make the offer for him. This messenger brought horses or other goods, spoke briefly with the parents, and left. To avoid embarrassment he did not immediately receive an answer. If the proposal was turned down, the horses were simply released and driven back to the suitor's herd; if accepted, the horses were taken into the father's herd, thereby announcing the engagement. Sometimes, a marriage was arranged with an older man of wealth, but girls resisted such unions, often eloping with the young men they truly loved.

The band might hold a wedding feast and dance, but often the young man simply took his bride to his tipi.

Death. Old men who no longer went on the warpath had a special tipi called the Smoke Lodge, where they gathered each day. A man typically joined when he became more interested in the past than in the present or future. Boys and women were not allowed inside, and new members underwent an initiation.

A very old and ill person was "thrown away" by everyone other than close family, not from a lack of sympathy, but out of a deep fear that evil spirits were invading his body. As death approached, the old person gave away his belongings, made his last medicine, then found a quiet place where he lay down and died.

Upon death, the body was immediately tended—the knees folded to the chest and the head tilted forward before the warmth had left the body. The body was bound in this position with a rope, then bathed. The face was painted red and the eyes sealed with clay.

The deceased was attired in the finest clothing available, then laid upon a blanket. Loved ones had a final look and then the body was wrapped in the blanket and bound with rawhide thongs. Placed in a sitting position on a horse, with a woman rid-

The deceased were most often buried in a sitting position and covered with rocks or sticks. Some Comanche, however, especially those along the Red River, placed the dead on scaffolds high in the trees.

This 1956 painting by Blackbear Bosin entitled And They Moved Without Him *depicts mourners pausing on horseback by the burial scaffold before they break camp and wander after the buffalo once again.*

ing behind, the body was taken to the burial place—usually a cave, deep ravine, or crevice high among the rocks.

The body was placed in a sitting position—or on its side—in a hole or on the ground, around which wooden poles and rocks were stacked. In the late 1800s, some Comanches, especially those living along the Red River, built tree or scaffold burials, like those used by the Cheyenne and other Plains Indians. The Comanche did not fear death, but the dead often worried them, and they often broke camp after a burial to get away from the place of death.

There was little mourning for old people who had died. But if a young man was killed, people grieved intensely for a long time—

the band depended upon young, strong warriors and hunters. Female relatives blackened their faces and put on rags. They wailed and gashed themselves with slivers of flint, keeping the wounds raw and painful for several months. Out of respect, the name of the deceased could not be mentioned.

Occasionally, they built a fire near the young man's grave, then danced and sang of the tragic loss. The family of the deceased gave away or destroyed their belongings and those of the dead. The young man's tipi was burned. Objects with strong medicine were thrown into the river or placed high in a tree.

People mourned intensely for three to fifteen days, often refusing to eat or leave the grave. Eventually, the grief subsided, but still the mourners might leave the camp briefly at sunrise or sunset, wandering away to think of their loved one. The grave was generally avoided, and if the band ever passed it again, they renewed their mourning.

Warfare

The Comanche regarded fighting as a noble pursuit and they often went to war seeking glory and goods, especially horses. They also sought to avenge friends and family killed in battle. The Comanche warriors were determined to hold the hunting grounds of the south plains and drive away other Native Americans, as well as Mexican and American settlers.

Warfare and raiding had long become a way of life. All men became warriors, and bravery and skill in battle were revered. To die young was glorious, it was believed, and spared one from the misery of old age. Through the entire course of their lives, from boyhood to old age, men were honored through a tribal system of rank and status based upon their heroism in battle.

Warriors received the greatest acclaim for individual acts of bravery, known as "counting coup." Men counted coup by touching an enemy during a fight. To shoot an enemy from a distance or to scalp a dead warrior was not as heroic or dangerous as rid-

In Comanche Scalp Dance, a 1962 painting by Leonard Riddles, a group of warriors celebrate another victory with fresh scalps dangling from their shields and spears.

leader "whose medicine was strong," or who was known for his skill and luck. These groups made hit-and-run raids on enemy camps to steal tethered horses—another way of counting coup—or to avenge a death.

Before going on the warpath, the leader made medicine to determine when and where the attack should take place. Then he called his friends and the older men into council. After eating, they smoked a pipe—those not wishing to join the party simply handed the pipe to the next person. If the leader was encouraged by these men, he daubed himself with warpaint and donned battle dress. During the afternoon, he drummed and sang war songs in his tipi. Then toward sundown the war party rode through the camp, asking others to join them; often, people turned out to sing and praise the warriors. After dark on the night before departure, a War Dance was held—or a Vengeance Dance, if the attack was to avenge a death—with drum beating, gourd rattling, and war whoops filling the air.

The Comanche did not need a dance to rouse their passion for combat. They were always ready for war. Yet warriors stilled missed loved ones left back at the camp, as expressed in this song:

> Going away tonight;
>> Be gone a long time.
> While I'm gone,
>> I'll be thinking of you.

their accuracy and distance. Men also played kickball and wrestled each other. However, unlike native peoples in eastern North America, they did not play stickball. Most of their contests—horseback riding, handling weapons, and fighting hand to hand—prepared them for a life as hunters, warriors, and raiders.

Women played a kind of kickball, as well as shinny and double ball. In shinny, which was similar to field hockey, women dressed up and divided into two teams on a playing field with stakes driven into the ground at either end. With curved sticks they struck at a deerskin ball stuffed with hair. The object of the game was to hit the stakes with the ball. Double ball was similar, except a rawhide thong about eighteen inches long was used instead of a ball. The game was played much faster too, as, catching the thong on their hooked sticks, the women raced down the field tossing it back and forth until they were close enough to make a good throw and wrap it around a stake.

Hand games, dice and, in later years, card games were played during hot weather and at night, as well as by those too old for athletics. Wooden cubes or plum stones painted on one side were used as dice. Players guessed and placed bets on which color would turn up when the cubes were flung onto the ground. Women enjoyed a similar kind of dice game played with plum stones tossed in a wicker basket. Men also played a game with two smooth sticks, about four inches long, flattened on one side and curved on the other. Holding the sticks between thumb and forefinger, the player dropped them on a buffalo skin. Points were earned depending on where the sticks landed. Women varied the game by using twelve sticks, six to ten inches long. Any sticks that crossed where they landed scored one point; the first player to get a hundred points won the game.

One of the most popular games was called by different names—bullet, button, or hands. Players formed two lines, facing each other. As they sang and beat out a rhythm on small drums or sticks, a player passed a button or other small object from hand to hand, and the opponent had to guess which hand held the object. Or the object was passed from one player to another, and the opposing team had to guess who ended up with it.

The Comanche so loved games and gambling that they often bet not only blankets and war clubs, but horses and tipis. Sometimes, they were impoverished by their passion for games of chance.

Making Meals

Although they never took part in armed conflict, women played an essential role in Comanche life. In addition to making and setting up the tipis, they undertook the arduous tasks of providing food and making meals for their families. The Comanche lived primarily on buffalo meat, but also hunted elk in the river valleys, black bears in the Cross Timbers, pronghorn antelope in the Llano Estacado, and deer wherever they came upon them. When game was scarce the men hunted wild mustangs, and when

The Comanche relied on the buffalo as their primary source of meat. Here, a warrior has separated a buffalo from the herd. On his swift, powerful horse, he gallops after the fleeing beast.

war parties did not have time to hunt, they would sometimes eat one of their ponies. In later years, the Comanche raided Texas ranches and stole longhorn cattle, whose meat tasted similar to buffalo. They did not eat fish or fowl; however, when starving,

After the women had made pemmican, they stored the special "energy food" in parfleches. Although the storage pouches had purely practical uses, they were sometimes fringed with buckskin and ornately decorated.

people ate virtually any creature they could catch, including armadillos, skunks, rats, lizards, frogs, and even grasshoppers.

In addition to preparing buffalo meat and other wild game, women gathered wild fruits, seeds, nuts, and berries. These included plums, grapes, juniper berries, persimmons, mulberries, and the fruit of the prickly pear cactus. They also collected acorns and pecans and dug roots and tubers—wild onions, radishes, and Indian potatoes, as well as Jerusalem artichokes and the bulbs of the sego lily. They acquired corn, dried pumpkin, and tobacco through trade and raids. Women used the berries and nuts, as well as honey and tallow, to flavor buffalo meat. They stored the tallow, or fat, in intestine casings or rawhide pouches called parfleches (PAR flesh es). They especially liked to make a sweet mush of buffalo marrow mixed with crushed mesquite beans.

The Comanches sometimes ate raw meat, especially raw liver flavored with gall. They also drank the milk from the slashed udders of buffalo, deer, and elk. Among their delicacies was the curdled milk from the stomachs of suckling buffalo calves. They also enjoyed buffalo tripe, or stomachs. Most meats were roasted over a fire or boiled. To boil fresh or dried meat and vegetables, women dug a pit in the ground, which they lined with animal skins or a buffalo stomach and filled with water to make a kind of cooking pot. They placed heated stones in the water until it boiled and had cooked their stew. After they came into contact with the Spanish, they traded for copper pots and iron kettles, which made cooking easier.

People generally had a light meal in the morning and a large evening meal. During the day, they ate whenever they were hungry, or when it was convenient. Like other Plains Indians, the Comanche were very hospitable. They prepared meals whenever visitors arrived in camp, which led to the belief that the Comanches ate at all hours of the day or night. Before eating at a public event, the chief took a morsel of food, held it to the sky, and then buried it as an offering to the Great Spirit. Many, but not all, families similarly offered thanks as they sat down to meals in their tipis.

Loved by the Comanches and other native peoples, pemmican was made by mixing dried meat with fruits, nuts, and berries. Wild cherries or plums, as well as pecans, walnuts, or piñon nuts were crushed and dried in the sun, then mixed with the pounded meat and some tallow or marrow fat. The pemmican was stored in parfleche bags, large intestines, or paunches, often with tallow poured over the container to make it airtight. With proper care, pemmican kept for years. Sliced and dipped in honey, traders loved pemmican, which they called "Indian bread." Children ate pemmican, but it was primarily a tasty, high-energy food reserved for war parties. Carried in a parfleche pouch it was only eaten, however, when the men did not have time to hunt. Similarly, in camp people ate pemmican only when other food was scarce.

Here's a modern version of pemmican that you can make at home:

Pemmican

Ingredients:

2 cups shredded beef or buffalo
1 cup dried red cherries, raisins,
    or other dried berries
6 tablespoons lard or butter

You can use either roast beef that has been well-cooked, or jerky made from beef or buffalo meat. Traditionally, jerky was made by hanging thin strips of meat on racks to dry in the sun for a week or so. You can make jerky by cutting buffalo or beef (preferably flank steak) into thin strips about 1/8 of an inch thick, five to six inches long, and three inches wide. Place the strips on a wire rack on a cookie sheet and bake at 150 degrees for about four to seven hours, depending on the thickness and moisture content of the strips. The jerky is ready when the meat is dry and flexible, but does not break.

To make pemmican, lightly pound the meat on a cutting board with a wooden mallet used for tenderizing meat. Next, pound the berries, then mix the meat and fruit with the softened butter, form into patties, place on a serving dish, cover with plastic wrap, and refrigerate until served.

Dress

Women made all the clothing for their families, most of which was plain and simple. Men wore a breechcloth—a strip of buckskin wrapped between their legs and tucked under a belt—along with fringed buckskin leggings and moccasins. Made from buffalo hide, the moccasins had large ankle flaps and long fringes along the heel and front seam. The flaps of their breechcloths were decorated front and back with shells and feathers. Men did not begin wearing shirts until they had met European traders, after which they began to favor shirts made from the tanned leather of deer, antelope, and mountain sheep. During warm weather, young boys went naked until they were nine or ten, at which point they began to dress like their fathers and the other men in the band. In winter, everyone wore knee-high boots and thick buffalo robes.

Men parted their long hair down the middle and often painted their scalps red or yellow along the part. They wore two braids at either side of the head and a braided scalp lock hung over the forehead. As decorations, they wrapped the braids with fur or cloth strips and tied bits of cloth, beads, and a yellow or black feather to their scalp locks. They usually plucked their facial and body hair—even their eyebrows—and adorned themselves with leather or metal armbands and earrings made of shells, brass, or silver.

When going to war, men painted their faces and covered their bodies with symbolic designs that gave them good medicine. Red was a highly favored color, but black, yellow, green, and blue were

*E*ntitled Little Spaniard, a Warrior, *this portrait by George Catlin shows a Mexican kidnapped as a boy, who became a great Comanche warrior. Here, he poses in traditional dress with weapons in hand.*

also used. They donned impressive headdresses of buffalo horns
and carried shields painted with geometric designs and fringed
with feathers that fluttered in the wind and threw off an enemy's
aim. A shield might also be adorned with bear teeth to show that
the man was a great hunter, scalps to indicate he was a brave warrior, and horse tails to suggest that he was a skilled raider. In the

This painting by Charles Marion Russell shows a Comanche war party poised to attack.

nineteenth century, eagle feathers replaced the buffalo horns on headdresses.

Women favored knee-length, fringed buckskin dresses with wide sleeves and flared skirts. Their moccasins were similar to those worn by the men. Sometimes, they decorated their dresses with painted designs and elk teeth, and after beads became available through trade, with bands of beadwork. Unlike the boys, young girls began to wear breechcloths as soon as they could walk and buckskin dresses when they reached puberty. For ceremonies, they wore fringed dresses highly adorned with beads and bits of iron or tin that chimed as they moved—today these dresses are called "tinklers." Unlike the men, who were quite vain about their hair, the women paid little attention to their hair, which they cut short or even hacked off. Women did part their hair and paint the part, but otherwise they let the strands hang loose. They lavishly painted their faces, however, circling their eyelids with red and yellow lines, painting their ears red, and daubing their cheeks with reddish orange circles or triangles.

Handicrafts

Because they traveled on horseback, dragging travois behind them, the Comanche did not have many belongings. Household goods had to be light and unbreakable since the Comanche were so frequently on the move. Women did not make pottery, which could be broken on their long journeys. Basketry, weaving, wood carving, and metalworking were also unknown among the Comanche. Instead they depended upon the buffalo for most of their tools, household goods, and weapons. Nearly two hundred different articles were made from the horns, hides, and bones of the buffalo. Removing the lining of the inner stomach, women made the paunch into a water bag. The lining was stretched over

*W*omen wore moccasins and long buckskin dresses with fringes, which protected their feet and legs as they made their way over the rough terrain of the southern plains.

Among the Comanche one of the most important household items was the parfleche. Food, clothing, and personal belongings were all stored in these handy pouches and packed on the travois.

Warriors used the thick, tough leather from the hump of an old buffalo bull to make their shields.

four sticks, then filled with water to make a pot for cooking soups and stews. With wood scarce on the plains, women relied on buffalo chips to fuel the fires that cooked meals and warmed the people through the long winters.

Stiff rawhide was fashioned into saddles, stirrups, cinches, and thongs, as well as knife cases, buckets, and moccasin soles. Rawhide was also made into rattles and drums. The thick neck skin of an old bull was ideal for war shields that deflected arrows as well as bullets. Strips of rawhide were twisted into sturdy ropes. Scraped to resemble white parchment, rawhide skins were folded to make parfleches in which food, clothing, and other personal belongings were kept. Women also tanned hides to make soft and supple buckskin, which was used for tipi covers, warm robes, blankets, clothes, and moccasins. They also relied upon buckskin for bedding, cradles, dolls, bags, pouches, quivers, and gun cases.

Sinew was used for bowstrings and sewing thread. Hooves were turned into glue and rattles. The horns were shaped into cups, spoons, and ladles, while the tail made a good whip, a flyswatter, or a decoration for the tipi. Men made tools—knives, scrapers, and needles—from the bones as well as a kind of pipe, and fashioned toys for their children. As warriors, however, men concentrated on making bows and arrows, lances, and shields. Since they spent most of each day on horseback, they also fashioned leather into saddles, stirrups, and other equipment for their lively mounts. Buffalo hair became a filler in saddle pads and was also plied into rope and halters.

4. Beliefs

To the Comanche, the sun and the moon were divine spirits, as were many of the animals that roamed the plains. But of all these, the earth was especially revered, viewed as the mother of the people.

PEOPLE BELIEVED IN THE GREAT SPIRIT, THE CREATOR OF THE UNIVERSE. The sun, moon, and earth were also supernatural beings, as were many animals. The sun, in particular, was honored as a powerful force, and the earth was addressed as Mother. Some people also believed in the Evil Spirit who struggled against the Great Spirit. Misfortune and disaster were the work of the Evil Spirit, while the Great Spirit bestowed good fortune on those who sought his blessings.

The religion of the Comanches was not highly organized, and they had few group ceremonies. Of the Plains Indians, they were one of the few peoples who did not celebrate the Sun Dance—only once did they come together for the dance, in 1873. Instead, they emphasized the medicine, or spiritual power, of the individual.

Medicine men did not lead religious societies, but served instead as healers. They treated physical illness and injuries, such as gunshot wounds and broken bones. They used tourniquets to stop the flow of blood and performed simple surgery. They relied upon a variety of herbal medicines to cure illnesses, protect people from evil, and guide people on their journeys of self-discovery.

To the Comanche, belief was a deeply personal matter between an individual and the spirits. Young men established their relationship with the spirits through the vision quest. Before embarking on this spiritual journey, a young man approached a medicine man who bathed him as an act of purification.

Wearing a breechcloth and moccasins and carrying only a buffalo robe, pipe, tobacco, and flint for lighting the pipe, the young man sought a nearby hill or other isolated place. Along the way, he halted four times to smoke the pipe filled with sacred tobacco and pray to the spirits. He remained on the hill for four days and nights without food or water, smoking the pipe and praying to the spirits. At night he wrapped himself in a buffalo robe and faced east. Come dawn, he prayed to the rising sun and throughout the day he basked in its rays.

When a youth embarked on a vision quest, he slept alone, often under a full moon. This was popularly known as a "Comanche moon," when warriors rode out on raids under the silver light.

*I*t was believed that spirits lived within the buffalo, perhaps because the vast herds were so essential to the survival of the Comanche. Sometimes, the buffalo spirits spoke to them or took on human form.

If a vision did not come to him, he would go on another quest. If he received a vision, he returned to the camp and asked the medicine man to interpret its meaning. The supernatural powers that came to the young man during the vision were potent—and sometimes dangerous. From the medicine man he also learned the sacred songs and magical medicines, and was warned of taboos, such as foods that must be avoided. He began to understand the special powers of animals, especially the buffalo, coyote, and eagle. He placed special charms—bear claws, feathers, and skins—in his medicine bundle. The medicine bundle embodied his strength in this world and his relationship with the supernatural, including his guardian spirit. Men needed great medicine if they were going to be victorious in battle and successful in hunting. Often, when seeking vengeance, going on a raid, or curing an illness, warriors sought visions to strengthen their medicine.

Not everyone possessed medicine of equal power. Some people enjoyed strong medicine while others had little. Those individuals with strong medicine were expected to share with others to benefit everyone in the band. They could not give away their medicine, but they could tell others how they might use a little of it. They felt obliged to be generous with their medicine; otherwise it would appear as if they really didn't have strong medicine after all. However, if shared with more than twelve people, the medicine became diluted and weak. A woman usually acquired her power, or medicine, through her husband; if he died in battle, she could assume his medicine to insure good fortune for the family.

The Comanche believe that the buffalo were once imprisoned by evil forces. There are many versions of the buffalo story, but all revolve around the herds being freed from captivity.

The buffalo became restless and scared; they milled about the pen. The puppy's howling awoke the old woman and her cousin. "Where is my pet?" asked the boy.

"There he is!" the old woman screamed. "I told you to get rid of that creature." She desperately tried to hold back the buffalo, but it was too late. The powerful beasts snorted, stamped the ground, and smashed through the pen. The grateful Comanche climbed onto their horses and raced after the thundering beasts. And this is how the buffalo came to roam freely over the broad plains, thanks to wise Coyote and his noisy pup of a cousin.

Ceremonies and Dances

The Comanche usually prayed to the Great Spirit privately, not in groups. But by the mid-1800s some bands had adopted group rituals, such as the Beaver Ceremony and the Eagle Dance. Likely borrowed from the Pawnee, the Beaver Ceremony was performed to cure illnesses. A large tipi was set up with trenches on either side that were filled with water to symbolize beaver ponds. Earthen mounds were shaped into beavers facing westward. There was also a pit over which an eagle feather dangled. A fire was started as the patient was brought into the tipi. Approaching from the east, the medicine man called others to join him, especially the sick or weak. Under his direction, drummers pounded out a rhythm, and people sang of beaver medicine. The medicine man next took a pipe and drew four puffs of smoke and prayed to

*S*ongs and dances were accompanied by the steady rhythm of drums. People sang of the power of beaver medicine, or danced with the courage and grace of the magnificent eagle.

*E*ntitled The Dancer, *this painting by Doc Tate Nevaquaya depicts a Comanche warrior dancing at a spiritual event–either an Eagle Dance or a Beaver Ceremony.*

heal all who had come together. This ceremony continued for two days and nights, ending at noon on the third day. The elaborate ritual in which they drew cures from sources deep within the earth—symbolized by the pit and the beaver—stood in contrast to the plain, straightforward everyday lives of the Comanche.

The Eagle Dance was held at the request of a man who sought powerful medicine for a son or nephew who was coming of age. He found a medicine man with strong eagle or war power, and offered him a pipe. If the medicine man accepted, he announced the day and place when the dancers would come together. In preparation, they bathed in a creek, dressed in their breechcloths, then adorned themselves with war paint and eagle feathers and rubbed themselves with sage. They sat down in a semicircle, facing east, and smoked tobacco. Then a leader, followed by the dancers, crept silently to a nearby camp and "captured" a girl—in the past, the girl really had to be a captive taken from an enemy village. The girl's family pretended to defend her, but the dancers won out and carried her back to their camp. As the girl sat beside the leader, the dancers stomped to the music of the drummers and singers. In his right hand, each dancer shook a rattle decorated with eagle feathers, beads, and paint. In his left hand, he carried a feathered wand or fan. The dancers represented young eagles soaring away from the nest. Although they did not sing, they occasionally cried out like the proud birds. Between dances, warriors rushed into the circle and boasted of brave coups. This was met with whoops, stomping feet, and shaking rattles. The stories had to be true because the eagle medicine was strong, and misfortune would befall anyone who exaggerated or told a lie.

About midmorning, one of the mothers brought fresh water to the thirsty dancers. Occasionally, the girl's family appeared and symbolically tried to recapture her but failed, after which they brought gifts. Friends and family of the dancers also contributed gifts, some of which were kept by the medicine man. Others were given to the dancers. Shortly before noon, the dance concluded, and the feathered wands and rattles were presented to the girl. The dancers raced to the stream and dove into the water four times, then dressed in their finest clothes and returned to camp for a great feast prepared by the women.

Faced with the loss of their lands and lifeways, many Comanches turned to the Ghost Dance Religion, which swept over the Great Plains toward the end of the nineteenth century. Wovoka, a Paiute, had a vision in which a new earth covered the land that had been damaged by the settlers. In his vision, the spirits of dead Indians and buffalo had also come back to the Plains. The Comanches first learned about the religion from the Cheyenne. They then held their own Ghost Dance, a solemn ceremony of despair over their long struggles. After many hours of dancing around a pole and chanting sad songs, many people fell to the ground in trances. They had visions of vast herds of buffalo, prong-horns, and their departed loved ones coming back to life. Yet, in the end, they were bitterly disappointed. A division called the Wasps were the only Comanches who remained converts to the new religion.

The Comanches practiced their traditional beliefs, including the Beaver Ceremony and Eagle Dance, until the 1890s when the Comanche leader Quanah Parker introduced the peyote religion. Confined to the reservation, people were comforted by coming together to sing, pray, and take peyote, a slightly hallucinogenic drug taken from a cactus plant. For hundreds of years, many Native Americans had taken the drug to induce visions that would help them find their spiritual path through life. By 1918, the peyote religion led to the formation of the Native American Church, which blended traditional beliefs with Christianity. Today, some Comanche people still belong to this church while most have joined various Christian denominations.

5. Changing World

This sketch shows Comanche warriors on their way to a council at Medicine Lodge Creek. Despite pressure from soldiers, the Comanche refused to surrender their homeland to settlers.

As they gradually moved southward, the Comanche drove out the other Plains Indians, including the Jicarilla Apaches. They also fought the Kiowa, but entered into a peace agreement with them in 1790, which has not been broken to this day. The Comanche did not encounter English-speaking traders until 1815. A few years later, in 1822, they entered into a trade agreement with General Thomas James, who mistook them for Pawnee. In 1834, the Comanche encountered the first official military expedition sent by the United States government. Holding council with these representatives and other Native American delegations, the Comanche signed their first treaty with the United States at Camp Holmes on the Canadian River in present-day Oklahoma in August 1835. Nearly twenty years passed before the southern bands of the Comanche were assigned to a reservation in north-central Texas, and most of the tribe eventually moved there.

As more settlers moved onto the southern plains or crossed the Comanche's hunting grounds on the way west, their way of life was greatly disrupted. Although the Comanche had entered into another peace treaty with the United States in 1853, only a few bands were represented. Most continued to battle settlers and soldiers, buffalo hunters and traders. The Comanche launched a series of raids and surprise attacks as they fiercely resisted the westward advance. In brutal retaliation, American soldiers and Texas militia, including the well-known Texas Rangers, slaughtered women and children, as well as countless warriors. It became clear that the goal of the United States government was

Quanah Parker, whose mother had been kidnapped and adopted by the Comanches, became one of their greatest chiefs. Yet despite Parker's keen intelligence and courage, the Comanches finally had to surrender when the buffalo neared extinction.

not simply to win the war but to annihilate the Comanche people. In the spring of 1858, Texas militia attacked a camp near the mouth of the Little Robe River and killed seventy-six people, including Chief Pohebits Quasho, also known as Iron Jacket. That same year, soldiers attacked an encampment on Rush Creek in Oklahoma—after the band there had just signed a peace treaty with the United States.

Confined to reservations, the Comanche had to accept handouts, such as this issue of clothing. Once free, they now depended on the U.S. government for food, clothing, and shelter.

Then, in 1859, the southern bands were forced to relocate from their reservation to Indian Territory in the present state of Oklahoma. There, under the watchful eye of government agents, they settled along the Washita River. Just after the Civil War, the remaining Comanche took part in peace councils and they, too, began to settle on reservations in 1868. Yet the raids and skirmishes continued as the Comanche proudly resisted settlers and soldiers. But the buffalo were vanishing from the prairies, adding to the hardships they faced. Led by Quanah Parker, the last of the Comanches remained in Texas and fought until June 24, 1875, when, weary and hungry, they finally surrendered at Fort Sill in present-day Lawton, Oklahoma.

The Comanche went on their last buffalo hunt in 1878. Thereafter, they began to raise cattle, although they did not like being confined to the reservation. Quanah Parker, the first official leader on the reservation, encouraged his people to adopt the new way of life as ranchers and farmers, but settlers continued to take the Comanche's land. The Dawes Act of 1901 formally broke up lands in Oklahoma, including those of the Comanche. Tribal lands were allotted to individuals, who were often cheated out of their small farms, and the remaining land was sold to settlers and speculators. The Comanche lost their land and their sovereignty as a nation. Their children were sent away to boarding schools, and people were pressured to abandon their traditional way of life. For many years, the Comanches struggled to keep their culture alive.

Language

Here are some examples of words from the Comanche language. These examples are based primarily on the *Comanche Vocabulary: Trilingual Edition*, compiled by Manuel García Rejón.

The consonants in the following words are similar to those in English. The vowel sounds are approximately *a* as in *father*, *e* as in *hey*, *i* as in *police*, *o* as in *note*, and *u* as in *rule*. If the letter is doubled, its sound is lengthened. Thus the *a* in *caani* (house) is held a little longer than the *a* in *pia* (mother). The *h* is always sounded as in English *hit*, even in the middle of a word, as in and *cuhtz* (buffalo). An accent mark indicates a stress, or emphasis, on that sound.

Many of these words from the Comanche language have been kept alive to the present day. Some of the words, such as *puc* (horse) and *cuhtz* (buffalo), have been especially important to traditional culture.

boy	tuinéhpua
brother (older)	bávi
brother (younger)	rámi
buffalo	cuhtz
corn	janib
cougar	toyarohco
coyote	tzensa
cricket	tuaahtaqui
deer	areca

dog	sarrie
father	ap
fire	cuuna
fish	pécui
frog	pasauiyió
grass	sonip
horse	puc
house	caani
jerky	inap
moon	muea
mother	pia
no	niatz
owl	mupitz
rabbit	tábo
rain	emar
rainbow	paracoa
river	piajunubi
sister (older)	batzi
sister (younger)	nami
sky	tomóbi
star	tatzinupi
sun	taabe
water	paa
yes	jaa

6. New Ways

Like other Native Americans, the Comanches enjoy coming together at powwows. Several are held each year in Oklahoma, such as the Comanche Nation Fair, in which these girls will be dancing.

THE COMANCHE HAVE NOT VANISHED FROM THE SOUTHERN PLAINS. THEY have since become a federally recognized tribe, the Comanche Nation, of about 11,500 people. The tribal government, with its headquarters in Lawton, Oklahoma, is popularly elected. Today, many Comanche live on their reservation near Lawton—one of the few nations who remain in the homeland of their ancestors. Some work on the reservation; others have jobs in nearby communities. Young people attend school in the area and are encouraged to learn about their ancestors' way of life.

Recently, tribal fairs, including powwows, have become a popular means of rekindling the fires of tradition. The powwow was once a spring event in which people came together to honor the seasonal renewal of life. People sang, danced, and prayed. Today, however, the Comanche powwow follows the same program used by Native American organizations throughout Oklahoma and in many other states. Families get together on a spring or summer weekend. There is a Grand Entry in which the Eagle staff, along with the American, state, and tribal flags are carried into the circle. Invited dignitaries and all the participants then dance clockwise around the circle. Accompanied by drum music and songs, the dancers then perform in different categories: men's traditional dance, men's grass dance, men's fancy dance, women's fancy dance, jingle dress dance, and intertribal dance. There are also songs and giveaways that hark back to the past, when a man donated horses, blankets, and other possessions to needy people in his band.

*H*ere, *three generations have come to the powwow–Marie Chebahtah,
her daughter Ann, and her grandson Jacob, who dances as a member of the
Comanche Ponies at the Comanche Nation Fair.*

Today, the Comanche no longer roam free across the stretches
of Texas prairie. Though many now work in offices and on farms,
unemployment remains high, and there is considerable poverty.
Much of the housing is also substandard, but the Comanches

have faith in themselves and their children. Over the years, they have devoted themselves to preserving the language, beliefs, and traditions of their ancestors. Despite their small population, the Comanche believe there will always be the triumphant cry of the Comanche warrior. They have endured waves of settlers, soldiers, and Texas Rangers, along with the harsh weather of the Great Plains. The Comanche know they will always have a place in the world. Just as the shaggy buffalo have returned to the plains from Texas to Canada, the words of the old Comanche song from the Plains Ghost Dance remind us:

> *Hi niswa vita ki ni*
> *Hi niswa vita ki ni*
>
> We are coming to life again.
> We are coming to life again.

Proud and skilled horsemen, the Comanche have faced unrelenting warfare and the near extinction of the buffalo. Yet the spirit of these warriors and hunters endures to this very day.

More About

the Comanche

Time Line

1519 Spanish introduce horses to North America.

about 1680 The Comanche acquire horses and learn to be expert riders.

about 1700 The Comanche split from the Shoshone and migrate from the mountains of present-day Idaho and Wyoming to the southern plains.

1720s The Comanche trade with the French for guns and other goods.

1725 The Comanche come to dominate the region that becomes known as the Comanchería (western Oklahoma, western Texas, and adjoining parts of Kansas, Colorado, and New Mexico.

1779 The Spanish, under the leadership of Don Juan Bautista de Anza, invade Comanche territory for the first time.

1781 Many women, men, and children die in a smallpox epidemic.

1786 The Comanche agree to end raids on the Spanish; trade is resumed between the two peoples.

1803 The United States purchases the Louisiana Territory from France, a vast area that includes part of the Comanchería.

1830 The Indian Removal Act is passed, forcing many eastern tribes to move to Indian Territory where the Comanche have long made their home.

1836 Texas wins independence from Mexico, prompting a new wave of Anglo settlers.

1840 When twelve Comanches, including Chief Muguara, are killed during the Council House Massacre, warriors raid homesteads in retaliation.

1845 Texas enters the Union, prompting another wave of Anglo settlers.

about 1850 Quanah Parker is born.

1867 A reservation is established for the Comanche in the Treaty of Medicine Lodge Creek.

1874 Many Comanches die in an attack on Adobe Walls in Texas, their last desperate attempt to drive the Americans out of the Comanchería.

1875 The last bands report to the reservation, thus bringing Comanche dominance of the southern plains to an end.

1880s Quanah Parker becomes principal chief. He raises badly needed funds for his people by leasing grazing rights on Comanche land to Texas ranchers.

1887 When the Allotment Act is passed the Comanche and other tribes in Oklahoma lose their tribal lands.

1900 Fewer than 1,000 buffalo remain on the Great Plains.

1907 Oklahoma, which includes most of the Comanchería, becomes a state.

1911 Quanah Parker dies and is buried next to his mother.

1934 The Indian Reorganization Act recognizes tribal governments and provides financial assistance.

1935 The impoverished Comanche receive financial assistance with the Oklahoma Indian Welfare Act, an initiative of President Franklin Roosevelt's New Deal program.

1966 The Comanche establish a tribal constitution under which a tribal council and business committee are formed.

1972 Comanche veterans of the Vietnam War establish the Little Ponies, an organization devoted to preserving native traditions.

Notable People

Buffalo Hump (active mid-1800s) proved himself a war chief in raids against Texans and Americans when he was still a young man. With about a thousand warriors, he raided Chihuahua, Mexico, stealing horses and taking captives as slaves. During the 1830s, he also led war parties against the Cheyenne and Arapaho, after which a lasting peace was established with these tribes and the Kiowa.

As chief of the Comanches, Buffalo Hump sought vengeance against the Texans after the Council House Massacre of 1840. In this incident, Texas Rangers captured some Comanche leaders under a flag of truce yet killed several of them. Buffalo Hump and his warriors swept through Texas, killing settlers and burning homesteads from north of the Red River to the Gulf of Mexico. Returning to the Comanchería, they were attacked by the Texas Rangers, but Buffalo Hump escaped with most of his men.

After a cholera epidemic raged through the southern plains in 1849, Buffalo Hump became principal chief. By the late 1850s, the Texas Rangers and the United States Army mounted a major offensive against the Comanches. In October 1858, Buffalo Hump's camp was attacked, and he lost three hundred horses. The Rangers also burned the tipis and the belongings abandoned on the plains by the Comanches.

At the end of the Civil War, in October 1865, Buffalo Hump joined other leaders of the southern Plains tribes in a meeting on the Little Arkansas River. They reluctantly agreed to give up their lands north of the river. However, warfare continued on the southern plains as Buffalo Hump's son, who took his father's name, and Quanah Parker continued to fight.

Buffalo Hump

LaDonna Harris

Cuerno Verde (died 1779), whose name means "green horn," frequently raided Spanish settlements along the Rio Grande in New Mexico in the 1770s. He seized food, horses, and captives. In order to bring peace to the region, Juan Bautista de Anza, the governor of New Mexico, led an attack on the Comanches in 1779. His force of 85 soldiers and 259 natives encountered Cuerno Verde in what is now Colorado. In the subsequent battle, Cuerno Verde and his son, along with a medicine man, four chiefs, and thirty-two warriors were killed.

LaDonna Harris (1931–   ) was born into a traditional Comanche household in Temple, Oklahoma. LaDonna spoke only Comanche until she started public school. During the 1960s, as wife of Senator Fred Harris of Oklahoma, she became active in a number of political causes. In 1965, she established Oklahomans for Indian Opportunity, a highly regarded self-help group. She has also chaired or served as a board member on numerous councils and committees. As a peace advocate, she has taken part in several international conferences.

Throughout her career, LaDonna Harris has been noted for promoting equality and self-determination for Native Americans.

Isatai (active 1870s) achieved fame among the Comanches when a comet appeared in 1874. He accurately predicted that the comet would vanish in five days and be followed by a long drought. He also claimed to have met with the Great Spirit who showed him how to make body paint that turned away bullets. He also predicted that a united uprising of Plains tribes would drive away settlers and soldiers, and that the buffalo would return to the grasslands. In 1874, he advised Quanah Parker to invite the Kiowa, Cheyenne, and Arapaho to a great Sun Dance in preparation for war.

However, in the Battle of Adobe Walls in Texas, Comanche attackers were soundly defeated. Armed with powerful Sharps and Remington rifles that were accurate over great distances, the buffalo hunters drove off the warriors. Thereafter, Isatai lost much of his prestige, but as late as 1890, he was still consulted by Quanah Parker.

Peta Nocona (Nokoni) (about 1815–1861), the father of Quanah Parker, led a band of Comanche raiders that was feared by Texans and Mexicans alike. In May 1836, he attacked Parker's Fort, a cluster of homesteads within a stockade. Among the five women and children taken captive was nine-year-old Cynthia Ann Parker who was adopted into the tribe and later became the wife of Peta Nocona.

Around 1850, Cynthia gave birth to Quanah Parker, who grew up to become the greatest of all Comanche leaders. In December 1860, while Peta Nocona and his warriors were away on a buffalo hunt, Texas Rangers attacked their camp and recaptured Cynthia. She tried to return to her husband, but was prevented by her parents. Peta Nocona never saw her again. He died about 1861 from a wound received in battle. She died three years later in 1864, it is said, of a broken heart.

Quanah Parker (about 1850–1911), the great Comanche leader, was born at Cedar Lake, Texas, the son of Peta Nocona and captive Cynthia Ann Parker. As he grew, Quanah, whose name means "fragrant" or "sweet smelling," came to excel as a hunter and warrior. He also demonstrated great leadership skills. When his parents died, Quanah grew to hate the whites. He became a war chief of the Comanche in the Texas Panhandle in 1867.

After the Civil War, the U.S. Army mounted an offensive to force the Plains Indians onto reservations. Under the Medicine Lodge Creek Treaty of 1867, a reservation was established for the Comanche and Kiowa in the southern part of present-day Oklahoma between the Washita and Red Rivers. However, Quanah and his band refused to give up their way of life. For the next seven years, they raided homesteads and frontier towns, and skirmished with the United States Army, then led by General William T. Sherman.

Although Quanah Parker was successful against the army, by the 1870s, the buffalo had nearly all been slaughtered, and the Comanche were going hungry. Then, in 1874, Quanah's band of seven hundred warriors was turned back at Adobe Walls in Texas by buffalo hunters armed with high-powered rifles. Finally, in June 1875, Quanah Parker and his band were forced to surrender to the army.

Quanah Parker settled in Indian Territory and became a prosperous farmer. Adopting his mother's name, he learned Spanish and English. Although he still loved the traditional Comanche way of life, he urged his people to adopt the new ways. Under his able leadership, the Comanche raised tribal revenues by leasing their grasslands to cattle ranchers. By 1890, Quanah Parker was the leader of all the Comanche bands. As a tribal delegate, he frequently traveled to Washington, D.C. He helped bring Geronimo back from Florida to the West by offering to share the Comanche reservation with the Apache prisoners. The two leaders rode together in the inaugural parade of Theodore Roosevelt.

When Quanah Parker died on February 23, 1911, he was buried next to his mother in Cache, Oklahoma.

Ten Bears (1792–1872), a renowned warrior of the Yamparika band, spoke eloquently for peace between the Indians and the settlers. In 1863, he traveled to Washington, D.C., as a tribal delegate but did not gain any consideration from the Comanches. In 1865, he signed a treaty on the Little Arkansas River in Kansas that established a reservation for the Comanches. Although he advocated peace, Ten Bears always distrusted whites. When he signed the Treaty of Medicine Lodge in 1867, Ten Bears recalled that he "was born where there were no enclosures and where everything drew a free breath. . . . I want to die there and not within walls." However, the Comanches were forced to surrender most of the lands—and their freedom—in exchange for a small reservation. In 1872, he again visited Washington, D.C., along with Tosawi and other delegates, but the government failed in its promises. Upon his return, Ten Bears was spurned by his own people, many of whom took up arms with Quanah Parker. Ten Bears died in despair at Fort Sill in Indian Territory.

Tosawi (active 1860–1870s), leader of the Penateka band, took part in numerous raids against Texas settlements in the 1860s. When the army responded by attacking the Comanches, Tosawi was one of the first leaders to surrender at Fort Cobb in Indian Territory. He told General Philip T. Sheridan, "Tosawi, good Indian." The general answered, "The only good Indians I ever saw were dead." This infamous reply is often misquoted as follows: "The only good Indian is a dead Indian." Tosawi traveled to Washington, D.C., with Ten Bears in an unsuccessful effort to negotiate better treaty terms for the Comanche.

Glossary

band A group of families who hunted, gathered, and traveled together, usually in their own territory.

breechcloth A cloth or skin worn between the legs; also breechclout.

burden carrier A wooden frame strapped to the back for carrying goods.

buckskin Deer hide softened by a tanning or curing process.

Comanchería Spanish word for the area of the Great Plains, including parts of Texas, Oklahoma, and Colorado, where the Comanche lived.

Comancheros Mexicans who traveled north to trade with the Comanche and other native peoples.

counting coup Striking an enemy in battle to prove one's bravery.

Ghost Dance A religion of despair that swept across the tribes of the Great Plains in the late 1800s.

Llano Estacado A broad plain encompassing west Texas from the Red River near the present-day border of Oklahoma nearly to the Mexican border.

moccasins Soft leather shoes often decorated with brightly colored beads.

nomadic Moving frequently from one place to another.

parfleche French word for a folded, rectangular-shaped, rawhide pouch for storing dried foods and belongings.

pemmican Pounded dry meat mixed with fat and berries used as "energy food" when warriors went on long journeys.

reservation Land set aside by the federal government as a home for Native Americans.

scalp The skin and hair from the skull of a defeated enemy.

skirmish A brief, minor fight, usually as part of an ongoing war.

sovereignty The right and ability of a people to govern themselves and their nation.

tipi A cone-shaped dwelling of the Comanche and other Plains peoples made with poles and a buffalo hide covering.

travois A sledlike carrier made of two poles and dragged by a dog or horse.

treaty A signed, legal agreement between two nations.

Tribal Council The legal governing body for the Comanche Nation.

vision quest A coming-of-age ceremony of solitary fasting for four days intended to induce dreams in young people.

Further Information

Readings

Over the years many fine books have been written about the Comanche. Among them, the following titles were consulted in researching and writing *The Comanche*.

"The Legend of the Bluebonnet" was adapted from a version by Mrs. Bruce Reid in J. Frank Dobie's *Legends of Texas*, published by the Texas Folklore Society in 1924. "The Coming of the Buffalo" was adapted from a story that appeared in *The Journal of American Folk-Lore*, Vol. XXII, July-September, 1909, Number LXXV.

Barnard, Herwanna Becker. *The Comanche and His Literature with an Anthology of His Myths, Legends, Folktales, Oratory, Poetry, and Songs.* Master's Thesis. University of Oklahoma, 1941.

Buller, Galen M. *Comanche Oral Narratives.* Doctoral Dissertation, University of Nebraska, 1977.

Curtis, Edward S. *The North American Indian: Being a Series of Volumes Picturing and Describing the Indians of the United States and Alaska.* New York: Johnson Reprint Corp., 1970.

Douglas, C. L. *The Gentlemen in the White Hats: Dramatic Episodes in the History of the Texas Rangers.* Austin, TX: State House Press, 1992.

Fehrenbach, T. R. *Comanches: the Destruction of a People.* New York: Knopf, 1974.

Griffin-Pierce, Trudy. *The Encyclopedia of Native America.* New York: Viking, 1995.

Hirschfelder, Arlene, and Martha Kriepe de Montaña. *The Native American Almanac: A Portrait of Native America Today.* New York: Prenctice-Hall, 1993.

Johansen, Bruce E., and Donald A. Grinde Jr. *The Encyclopedia of Native American Biography*. New York: Henry Holt and Co., 1997.

Johnson, Michael G. *The Native Tribes of North America: A Concise Encyclopedia*. New York: Macmillan Publishing Co., 1994.

Langer, Howard J., ed. *American Indian Quotations*. Westport, CT: Greenwood Press, 1996.

Malinowski, Sharon, and Anna Sheets. *The Gale Encyclopedia of Native American Tribes*. Detroit: Gale Research, 1998.

Malinowski, Sharon. *Notable Native Americans*. Detroit: Gale Research, 1995.

Rejón, Manuel García, and Daniel J. Gelo. *Comanche Vocabulary: Trilingual Edition*. Austin: University of Texas Press, 1995.

Shanks, Ralph, and Lisa Woo Shanks. *The North American Indian Travel Guide*. Petaluma, CA: Costano Books, 1993.

Waldman, Carl. *Encyclopedia of Native American Tribes*. New York: Facts on File Publications, 1988.

Wallace, Ernest, and E. Adamson Hoebel. *The Comanches: Lords of the South Plains*. Norman, OK: University of Oklahoma Press, 1952, 1986.

Young people who wish to learn more about the Comanche will enjoy these excellent books:

Alter, Judy. *The Comanches*. New York: Franklin Watts, 1994.

De Paola, Tomie. *The Legend of the Bluebonnet: An Old Tale of Texas*. New York: Putnam and Grosset Group, 1996.

Hilts, Len. *Quanah Parker*. San Diego: Harcourt Brace Jovanovich, 1987.

Lodge, Sally. *The Comanche*. Vero Beach, FL: Rourke Publications, 1992.

Marrin, Albert. *Plains Warrior: Chief Quanah Parker and the Comanches*. New York: Atheneum Books for Young Readers, 1996.

Mooney, Martin J. *The Comanche Indians.* New York: Chelsea House, 1993.

Rollings, Willard H. *The Comanche.* New York: Chelsea House, 1989.

Schwartz, Michael. *LaDonna Harris.* Austin, TX: Raintree Steck-Vaughn, 1997.

Organizations

Comanche Tribe
Wallace Coffey, Chairman
P.O. Box 908
Lawton, OK 73502
(405)492-3751 FAX 492-4981

Websites

Here are some of the best and most interesting websites you might like to visit for more information about the Comanche and other native peoples.

Comanche Sites:

The Comanche Language and Cultural Preservation Committee
http://www.skylands.net/users/tdeer/clcpc/

Comanche Literature
http://www.indians.org/welker/comanche.htm

Comanche Tribe of Oklahoma Education Programs
http://www.lawtonnet.com/com-ed/

Other Native American Sites:

Betnet Native American Sites
http://www.betnet.com/Indian.htm

First Nations: Histories
http://www.dickshovel.com/Compacts.html

FirstNations.com
http://www.firstnations.com/

Index of Native American Resources on the Internet
http://hanksville.org/misc/NAresources

Native American Navigator
http://www.ilt.columbia.edu/k12/naha/nanav.html

Native American Sites
http://www.pitt.edu/~lmitten/indians.html

Native Americans
http://www.americanwest.com/pages/indians.htm

NativeWeb
http://www.nativeweb.org/

Index

Page numbers for illustrations are in **boldface**.

Raymond Bial

HAS PUBLISHED OVER THIRTY CRITICALLY ACCLAIMED BOOKS OF PHOTOGRAPHS for children and adults. His photo-essays for children include *Corn Belt Harvest, Amish Home, Frontier Home, Shaker Home, The Underground Railroad, Portrait of a Farm Family, With Needle and Thread: A Book About Quilts, Mist Over the Mountains: Appalachia and Its People, Cajun Home,* and *Where Lincoln Walked.*

He is currently immersed in writing *Lifeways*, a series of books about Native Americans. As with his other work, Bial's deep feelings for his subjects is evident in both the text and illustrations. He travels to tribal cultural centers, photographing homes, artifacts, and surroundings and learning firsthand about the national lifeways of each of these peoples.

A full-time library director at a small college in Champaign, Illinois, he lives with his wife and three children in nearby Urbana.